Rinat Faritovich Burnashev

PHILOSOPHICAL ANALYSIS OF PERSONAL INFORMATION SECURITY

Rinat Faritovich Burnashev

PHILOSOPHICAL ANALYSIS OF PERSONAL INFORMATION SECURITY

IN THE INFORMATION SOCIETY Monograph

ScienciaScripts

Imprint

Any brand names and product names mentioned in this book are subject to trademark, brand or patent protection and are trademarks or registered trademarks of their respective holders. The use of brand names, product names, common names, trade names, product descriptions etc. even without a particular marking in this work is in no way to be construed to mean that such names may be regarded as unrestricted in respect of trademark and brand protection legislation and could thus be used by anyone.

Cover image: www.ingimage.com

This book is a translation from the original published under ISBN 978-620-7-65235-8.

Publisher:
Sciencia Scripts
is a trademark of
Dodo Books Indian Ocean Ltd. and OmniScriptum S.R.L publishing group

120 High Road, East Finchley, London, N2 9ED, United Kingdom
Str. Armeneasca 28/1, office 1, Chisinau MD-2012, Republic of Moldova, Europe
Printed at: see last page
ISBN: 978-620-7-89190-0

Rinat Faritovich Burnashev

PHILOSOPHICAL ANALYSIS OF INFORMATION security of a person in the information society

MONOGRAPHY.

Samarkand 2024

UDK 1(091) + (316.6)
BBK: 87.6

Burnashev R.F. Philosophical analysis of information security of the individual in the information society. - 2024. - 62 c.

The monograph is devoted to the study of philosophical aspects of personal protection in the global information space. The author considers the key concepts of information security through the prism of philosophy, analysing the impact of information technologies on human consciousness and identity.

The paper exposes the issues of privacy, digital identity and ethical dilemmas arising from technological advances.

Particular attention is paid to the issues of information culture and the development of regulatory frameworks that promote the protection of personal data and the sustainable development of the information society.

The monograph is of interest to specialists in philosophy, sociology, information technology, as well as all those interested in the problems of information security in the modern world.

Information security is the state of protection of information and supporting infrastructures from various threats, ensuring confidentiality, integrity and availability of information. It includes measures aimed at protecting data from unauthorised access, use, disclosure, destruction, alteration or destruction.

With the rapid development of information technologies and the digitalisation of all spheres of life, the problem of information security is becoming increasingly important. Modern society, which relies on information as a key resource, faces many threats related to cyberattacks, data privacy breaches and information manipulation. Insufficient information security can lead to serious economic, political and social consequences [1].

Information technologies significantly change not only social structures, but also human personality itself. Constant connection to the Internet, active use of social networks and mobile devices change the perception of the world, communication practices and even cognitive processes. At the same time, the vulnerability of the individual to information threats such as cyberbullying, leakage of personal data, and manipulation of consciousness through media and social networks is increasing.

The main objective of this study is to provide an in-depth philosophical analysis of the phenomenon of personal information security in the context of information society. The study aims to identify the fundamental problems and challenges faced by the individual in the context of information threats, as well as to develop a theoretical framework for understanding and ensuring information security. The main objectives of the study include:

1. Study of historical and theoretical aspects of the development of

the concept of information security.

2. Examination of philosophical approaches to the concept of information and security, their evolution and current discourses.

3. Identification of the main types of threats to personal information security in modern society.

4. Analysing psychological, social and ethical aspects related to information threats.

5. A study of personal information security strategy, including governmental, international and technological measures.

6. Identifying the role of education and culture in the formation of information literacy and increasing the level of information security of the individual.

Chapter I. Theoretical Foundations of Personal Information Security

Personal information security is a set of measures and strategies designed to protect personal data from unauthorised access, theft, leakage and other forms of misuse.

This chapter reviews the theoretical foundations of personal information security, which are the foundation for understanding and developing effective methods of protection. It is important to emphasise that information security includes not only technical aspects, but also legal, social and psychological components.

1.1. Historical aspects of the development of the concept of information security

The concept of **information security has travelled a** long way in its development due to changes in technology and social structures. In the beginning, information security referred exclusively to the protection of secret and confidential information in the military and governmental spheres. With the development of computing technology and the appearance of the first computers in the middle of the 20th century, the concept expanded to include the protection of data from unauthorised access and damage.

In the 1970s and 1980s, with the advent of personal computers and local area networks, there was a need to protect data in the commercial and private sectors. During this period, the first anti-virus programmes and access control systems began to be developed. In the 1990s, with the advent of the internet and the global network, information security became a key issue for all users, not just specialised organisations. New challenges emerged, such as cyber attacks, viruses, hacker attacks and data breaches.

In the 21st century, with the development of cloud technologies, mobile devices and the Internet of Things (IoT), information security has become even more complex. It now includes not only technical, but also organisational, legal and ethical aspects aimed at protecting personal data, intellectual property and critical infrastructure.

Let's look at some historical examples of information security threats.

1. *Morris worm* or *Internet worm 2 November 1988 was* one of the first widely known incidents when a network worm created by student Robert Morris spread across the Internet, infecting computers and causing serious problems with their operation [2]. This was due to a software bug that caused the worm to copy itself to other computers without the users' permission. This was an important event in the history of information security that highlighted the vulnerabilities of the new networking technology. After this incident, Morris was recognised as the first person in the US to be charged with violating the Computer Fraud and Abuse Act.

The Morris worm was a significant event in the history of computer security because it exposed vulnerabilities in network systems and brought attention to the need for security in network environments. The aftermath of the incident also led to the creation of CERT (Computer Emergency Response Coordination Centre) and increased efforts to secure networks.

2. *The attack on Yahoo,* which occurred in 2013-2014, is recognised as one of the largest in the history of the Internet, when approximately three billion user accounts were stolen. As a result of this attack, attackers gained access to personal information, including users' names, email addresses, phone numbers, dates of birth, and encrypted passwords [3].

This attack did not come to light until 2016, when Yahoo announced that it had experienced a major security breach that occurred in 2014. This was a major blow to Yahoo, and it caused changes in security policy and information management at the company. The attack also brought attention to cybersecurity issues and caused many companies to rethink their defences against cyber threats.

3.   The 2014 ***attack on Sony Pictures Entertainment*** was one of the most serious cybersecurity incidents ever seen in the entertainment industry. In late November 2014, a hacker group calling itself Guardians of Peace (GOP) attacked Sony Pictures' computer systems and stole a vast amount of sensitive information, including emails, financial data, behind-the-scenes documents about films, and personal information about employees [4].

The most notorious aspect of this attack was the disclosure of confidential correspondence between Sony Pictures employees, including the company's top management and well-known Hollywood personalities. This correspondence was not only unwanted by the company, but also attracted media attention due to the content of a number of racist and unprofessional comments.

The attack on Sony Pictures has had serious consequences for the company, including financial losses, data breaches and damage to its reputation.

4.***The WannaCry cyberattack of*** May 2017 was one of the most destructive and widespread cyber incidents in history. WannaCry exploited a vulnerability called EternalBlue that was found in Windows operating systems, which allowed WannaCry to spread across networks, infecting computers without user involvement [5].

After infecting a computer, WannaCry encrypted the data on the hard drive, making it inaccessible to the user. A message was then displayed demanding a ransom to decrypt the data. The attackers demanded that affected organisations and individuals pay a ransom in bitcoins to recover the data. This was one of the first major use cases of ransomware tactics in cyberattacks.

WannaCry infected hundreds of thousands of computers in more than 150 countries in just a few days. Government organisations, companies, banks, and medical facilities were affected, causing serious operational problems for some of them. Following the attack, Microsoft released a security update that closed the vulnerability and also provided patches for outdated versions of Windows, including Windows XP. The WannaCry attack stood out for its scale, rapid spread and serious consequences, emphasising the importance of cybersecurity and information technology governance.

These examples show that information security threats have been around for a long time and have evolved with technology. They emphasise the importance of continuous improvement of information security measures and the need to be aware of potential risks at both personal and corporate levels.

1.2. PHILOSOPHICAL APPROACHES TO THE CONCEPTS OF INFORMATION AND SECURITY

Information is a key category in modern philosophy, encompassing various aspects of human knowledge, communication and being. Philosophers consider information as a fundamental element of reality, along with matter and energy. It can be defined as any meaningful message that reduces uncertainty in the recipient. In a philosophical context, information includes data, knowledge, symbols and signs, which play a crucial role in the perception and interpretation of the world.

Consideration of information as a philosophical category includes several key aspects, each of which reveals different facets of its nature and significance.

The semantic aspect focuses on what exactly information conveys, its content and meaning. Here the issue of interpretation becomes important, i.e. how information is understood and comprehended by the subject. In the philosophy of language and information theory, semantics studies how symbols and signs relate to objects and phenomena of the real world.

The meaning of information can depend on the *context* in which it is used. The same sign or message can have different meanings depending on the situation.

The syntactic aspect deals with the formal structure of information, its organisation and the rules of combining symbols and signs. This aspect is most important in mathematics, computer science and linguistics, where the laws and principles of information structures are studied without regard to their meaning.

Syntax includes rules of grammar, programming logic, and any other *formal systems* that define how information should be organised and presented.

The pragmatic dimension looks at how information is applied in practice, its usefulness and its impact on the behaviour and decisions of actors. It examines the effectiveness, relevance and efficiency of information.

Pragmatics studies how information *influences* people's choices, behaviours and actions and includes the analysis of communicative acts, decision-making processes and the practical implementation of information.

These aspects are inextricably linked. For example, in order for information to be useful (pragmatic aspect), it must not only be properly organised (syntactic aspect), but also comprehended and interpreted (semantic aspect). The philosophical study of information helps to better understand its nature, role and significance in various contexts of human activity and cognition.

In philosophy, information is also analysed through the lens of various concepts, such as Claude Shannon's information theory, which focuses on the quantitative measurement of information and its transmission through communication channels, and Gregory Bateson's information theory, which views information as "the difference that matters" [6].

Security as a philosophical category also has many dimensions and interpretations. Several main theories can be distinguished in the philosophy of security [7].

1. *Classical security theory* is a set of principles and approaches that have developed in traditional political thought and international relations to ensure the defence of the state against external and internal threats. Let us take a closer look at the main elements of this theory.

Realism. The central premise of realism is that the international system is anarchic, that is, there is no supreme governing body over sovereign states. States operate under conditions of self-determination, seeking to ensure their own security and national interests. In anarchy, states seek to maintain a balance of power to avoid domination by one power over others. This may include the formation of alliances and coalitions as well as an arms race. States are seen as rational actors who make decisions based on analysing risks and benefits to ensure their own security.

Military security. Classical security theory places great emphasis on military power as the main means of defending the sovereignty and territorial integrity of a state. The presence of a strong army and defence structures serves as a deterrent to potential aggressors, reducing the likelihood of attack.

Sovereignty and territorial integrity. An important principle is the defence of the sovereignty and territorial integrity of a state against external encroachments. Recognition of international boundaries and rejection of forcible changes of territories are basic elements of international law and order.

Diplomacy and Negotiation. Despite the focus on military power, classical security theory recognises the importance of diplomacy and negotiation as means of resolving international conflicts. An important element is a pragmatic approach to negotiation, where each side seeks to maximise its benefits but is willing to compromise to ensure stability and prevent war.

Classical security theory, being based on the principles of realism, remains relevant in the modern world despite the emergence of new challenges and threats such as terrorism, cyber threats and environmental issues. Modern approaches to security often integrate classical principles with new concepts in order to adequately respond to changes in the international environment.

2. *Critical security theory* offers an alternative perspective on security issues that differs from traditional approaches such as realism. It develops within the framework of critical theory and poststructuralism, and focuses on a broader and more comprehensive understanding of security, including social, political and economic aspects. Let us take a closer look at the main elements of critical security theory.

Expanding the concept of security. In contrast to classical security theory, where the central object of security is the state, critical theory looks at security at the level of individuals, communities and international structures. Critical theory includes non-conventional threats such as economic instability, social inequality, environmental crises, pandemics and humanitarian problems in its analyses.

Deconstructing traditional concepts. Critical security theory is concerned with analysing how the notion of security is constructed through language, political discourses and practices. This includes examining who and how defines what constitutes a threat and what measures are considered legitimate to address it. An important aspect is to analyse the relationship between power and knowledge, identifying how certain forms of knowledge and understandings of security support existing power structures and hierarchies.

Empowerment and social justice. Critical security theory emphasises the protection of human rights and security at the level of individuals and communities. An important element is the endeavour to protect the interests of vulnerable groups that are often overlooked by traditional approaches to security.

Normative orientation. Critical security theory often raises questions of ethics and morality, seeking a more just and humane approach to security issues. A core principle is the pursuit of social justice and equality, which requires a rethinking of existing institutions and policies.

Globalisation and Intersectionality. Critical security theory examines the impact of globalisation on security, including the interconnections between different regions and actors in the global arena. An important element is to analyse how different forms of oppression and discrimination (e.g. gender, race, class) intersect and affect security.

Transformation and change. Critical security theory supports active social movements and initiatives aimed at structural change and improving security conditions for all sectors of society. An important element is the development and promotion of alternative security strategies that are based on the principles of cooperation, dialogue and peaceful conflict resolution.

Critical security theory seeks a more inclusive and equitable understanding of security that takes into account the complex and multidimensional aspects of human existence and interaction in a global context.

3. The *phenomenological approach to security* proposes to view security in terms of the experience and perception of actors, emphasising the subjective understanding and experience of security. This approach moves away from objectivist and structural models towards a more individualised and contextual understanding of security. Let us consider the main elements of the phenomenological approach.

Subjective perceptions of security. The phenomenological approach emphasises how individuals perceive and experience security or threat, which includes an examination of their feelings, thoughts and experiences in different situations. An important element is the consideration of the existential aspects of security related to feelings of safety, stability and confidence in the world.

Contextuality and situationality. Security is seen as a context- and situation-specific phenomenon, which includes social, cultural, economic and political factors that influence perceptions of security. Understanding that perceptions of security can vary according to time and place, as well as personal experiences and events in the subject's life.

Intersubjectivity. The phenomenological approach emphasises the importance of intersubjectivity, that is, the shared and mutual perception of security. This means that the understanding of security is formed through interaction with and perception of others. Security is understood as a socially constructed phenomenon where collective meanings and values play a key role.

Historicity. An important aspect is to consider the temporal dimension of security, how past, present and future events influence perceptions of security. Understanding how historical events and collective memory influence contemporary perceptions of security.

The phenomenological approach to security offers a deeper and more multidimensional understanding of the phenomenon, based on subjective experience and perception. This approach allows individual differences and contextual specificities to be taken into account, making it useful for analysing complex and dynamic security situations.

4. The existential ***approach to security is*** based on the philosophy of existentialism and focuses on the experiences, meanings and existential aspects of human life related to security. This approach focuses on the

internal, personal and existential aspects of security, considering it as a fundamental condition for the existence and self-realisation of an individual. Let us consider the main elements of the existential approach to security.

Existential security. The existential approach considers security as a basic condition for human existence. A sense of security allows people to feel their connection to the world and their place in it. The issue of security is seen as part of the existential struggle for existence, where threats can call into question the very possibility of being.

Existential anxiety is a fundamental feeling associated with the realisation of the finitude of human existence and vulnerability to nothingness. Security, in this context, is understood as a way of mitigating or overcoming this anxiety. Existential anxiety can stimulate a search for meaning and ways of defence, both physical and psychological.

Freedom and responsibility. The existential approach emphasises the freedom and responsibility of each individual to create their own safe space. This includes personal choices and actions to ensure one's own safety and the safety of loved ones. The individual is responsible for his or her own being and should actively participate in creating conditions conducive to a sense of safety.

Authenticity. The existential approach sees authenticity as an important aspect of security, which means living in accordance with one's own values and beliefs and creating an inner sense of security and wholeness. Authenticity requires a willingness to come into conflict with reality, including recognising and accepting the vulnerability and finitude of one's existence.

Interpersonal relationships. The existential approach emphasises the importance of interpersonal relationships for feeling safe. Support and acceptance from loved ones create a sense of security. Feelings of love, friendship and solidarity contribute to a sense of security and overcoming existential anxiety [8].

Meaning and purpose. Existential philosophy states that security is related to the search for and finding meaning in life. Awareness of meaning helps to cope with uncertainty and threats. Having clear goals and aspirations gives structure and direction to life, which contributes to a sense of security.

An existential approach to security offers a deep and personal understanding of the phenomenon, focusing on the inner experiences and meanings that people attach to their existence. This approach helps to take into account individual differences and existential aspects of human life, making it valuable for analysis and practical application in a variety of security-related contexts.

5. The ***concept of personal information security*** combines philosophical ideas about information and security, applying them to the conditions of the information society [9]. The main elements of this concept include:

Privacy is the protection of personal data and information from unauthorised access. In a philosophical context, privacy is related to the right to privacy and personal space.

Integrity - ensuring that information is reliable and immutable. Integrity of information is important for maintaining truth and trust in society.

Accessibility - the ability to receive information at the right time and place. Accessibility of information ensures freedom of speech and the right to be informed.

The philosophical concept of personal information security also includes an analysis of ethical issues such as the right to information, the balance between security and freedom, and the impact of information technology on personal identity and fulfilment. It is also important to consider the impact of globalisation and digitalisation on perceptions of security and privacy, and to explore information protection mechanisms that can contribute to the creation of a secure information environment for each individual.

1.3. INFORMATION SECURITY IN THE CONTEXT OF CONTEMPORARY PHILOSOPHICAL DISCOURSES

Postmodernism as a philosophical movement questions metanarratives and absolute truths, emphasising the multiplicity and fragmentation of reality. In the context of information security, the postmodernist approach emphasises the following aspects:

Deconstruction of truth. In postmodern discourse, information is perceived as a construct subject to manipulation and interpretation. Information security becomes not only a technical problem, but also a semantic one, where it is important to take into account who and how information is interpreted.

Plurality of perspectives. Postmodernism argues that there is no single correct point of view and this means that approaches to information security can differ depending on the cultural, social and political context.

Simulacra and hyperreality. Jean Baudrillard introduces the concept of hyperreality, where the boundaries between the real and the virtual are blurred. In this context, information security should take into account the phenomenon of fake news and simulacra, which create a false reality and affect the perception of truth [10].

Phenomenology, as a philosophical approach, emphasises the subjective experience and perception of the world by an individual. In the context of information security, phenomenological analysis includes:

Subjective perception of security. An important aspect is how an individual feels his/her security in the information space, which includes personal experiences and emotions related to threats to information security.

Live Experience and Interactivity. Phenomenology looks at how humans interact with information technology and how these interactions shape feelings of safety or insecurity.

Intentionalism and information flows. From a phenomenological perspective, it is important how the directionality of consciousness (intensionalism) influences information perception and decision-making and this helps to understand how information threats affect the daily life and actions of an individual.

Critical theory, from the Marxist tradition, seeks to expose structures of power and inequality by focusing on social and political aspects. In the context of information security, the critical approach considers:

Power and Control. Critical theory analyses how power is distributed through the control of information and this includes issues of censorship, surveillance and the management of information flows.

Ideology and manipulation. Critics draw attention to how information is used to manipulate public consciousness and reinforce existing power structures. An important aspect is to expose false narratives and propaganda.

Social justice and human rights. Critical theory emphasises the need to protect rights to privacy and access to information and this includes combating digital inequalities and protecting vulnerable groups from information threats [11].

Postmodernism, phenomenology and critical theory provide diverse and insightful approaches to analysing personal information security in the information society. They help to understand the multilayered and multivalent nature of information security problems and offer different strategies to address them, taking into account both objective and subjective aspects of this complex and important problem.

The study of the theoretical foundations of personal information security allows to form a holistic understanding of the problems and solutions in this area. Realising the importance of personal data protection and implementing effective security measures contributes to the creation of a safe and trusted digital environment for each individual.

CHAPTER II. THREATS TO PERSONAL INFORMATION SECURITY IN THE INFORMATION SOCIETY

Personal information security is an important aspect of modern human life, because with the development of technology and Internet resources, the number and variety of threats to personal information is rapidly increasing. Protection of personal data and ensuring confidentiality become priority tasks in the conditions of everyday use of online services, social networks and electronic means of communication. Various threats can negatively affect personal and financial security, reputation and psycho-emotional state of a person [12].

2.1. TYPES of THREATS TO PERSONAL INFORMATION SECURITY

Cyberattacks are targeted actions aimed at disrupting computer systems, networks and software. The main types of cyber attacks include viruses, Trojans, phishing, DDoS attacks, hacking and rootkits. The impact of cyber attacks on an individual can be multifaceted.

Financial losses from cyberattacks can be significant and vary depending on the type of attack, the size of the organisation and the industry. Consider the types of cyberattacks and the losses associated with them [13].

Ransomware attacks. Financial losses are related to ransom payments, data recovery, and downtime. For example, the attack on Colonial Pipeline in 2021, where ransom payments totalled about $4.4 million and total losses were estimated in the tens of millions of dollars [14].

Phishing. Financial losses are related to theft of funds, data leakage, reputation restoration. For example, in 2020 Twitter was attacked, which led to the hacking of high-ranking users' accounts and financial losses due to a decrease in customer trust [15].

DDoS attacks (distributed denial of service attacks). Financial losses are observed due to service downtime, loss of revenue from customers, and defence costs. In 2016, a DDoS attack on Dyn caused outages on major sites such as Twitter, Netflix, and Reddit, with estimated losses in the millions of dollars [16].

Data theft and security breaches. Financial losses include loss of sensitive information, fines and lawsuits, and security remediation. The Equifax hack in 2017, when 147 million people's data was stolen, cost the company more than $1.4 billion [17].

Financial losses from cyberattacks are a significant threat to businesses and the wider economy. Organisations must invest in cybersecurity, risk insurance and employee training to minimise these risks.

Psychological stress from cyberattacks is significant and can affect both individual users and employees of organisations. Let's look at the key aspects related to psychological stress caused by cyberattacks.

Fear and anxiety. Loss of personal information, the threat of further attacks, and uncertainty about the security of one's data lead to constant anxiety, fear of using digital devices, and insomnia.

Feelings of helplessness. Lack of control over the situation, the inability to prevent or stop the attack provokes depression, a feeling of loss of control over life, and decreased self-confidence.

Anger and frustration. Disruption of normal life or work, the need for costs to restore data or systems contribute to aggressive behaviour, irritability, feelings of injustice.

Post-traumatic stress disorder. The severe stress of an attack, especially if the incident was large-scale or had lasting consequences causes intrusive thoughts about the event, digital avoidance, and severe anxiety when using computers or internet services.

Stressed employees often lose the ability to concentrate, leading to decreased productivity, increased errors, which can exacerbate the effects of an attack. Executives and business owners may experience additional stress due to the responsibility of protecting the company and its data. The realisation of financial losses and possible legal implications can weigh heavily on the psyche.

Cyberattacks not only cause financial damage, but also have a significant impact on people's psychological well-being. Organisations must take this aspect into account and implement strategies to reduce stress and increase the psychological resilience of employees and managers.

Reputational damage from cyber-attacks is a major threat to companies and organisations. Reputational losses can be long-lasting and costly, affecting the trust of customers, partners and investors. Let's look at the key aspects and consequences of reputational damage from cyberattacks.

Loss of customer trust. Personal data leakage, clients' financial information becomes available to attackers, so clients may refuse from the company's services, switch to competitors, speak negatively about the company in social networks and forums.

Negative media coverage. Large-scale or high-profile attacks attract the attention of the media, which actively cover the incident, and negative publications can become permanently entrenched in the information field, affecting the perception of the brand.

Loss of business reputation. Partners and counterparties may doubt the reliability of the company as a business partner, which may lead to the termination of business relations, refusal to conclude new contracts, and deterioration of the terms of co-operation.

Falling share price. Investors react to data leaks and cyberattacks by selling company shares due to concerns about the company's future, which may lead to a decrease in the company's market capitalisation, reducing its investment appeal.

Reputational damage from cyberattacks can have a lasting and devastating impact on a company. However, a swift and transparent response, compensation for victims, improved security measures and proactive public relations can help mitigate the negative impact and restore brand trust.

Social engineering and manipulation are techniques used by attackers to deceive people and gain confidential information or access to systems. These methods rely on psychological techniques that influence people's behaviour and perceptions [18]. Let's look at the main aspects of social engineering and manipulation, as well as ways of defence.

Phishing. Sending fake emails or messages that look like official requests from trusted sources with the purpose of obtaining logins, passwords, financial information.

Smishing (SMS phishing). Sending text messages from fraudulent requests or links are used to install malware on your device.

Vishing (voice phishing). The use of phone calls to trick people into obtaining confidential information to obtain passwords, bank card numbers, and other personal information.

Pretexting. Creating a fictitious scenario or false story to obtain information in order to gain trust and extract sensitive data.

Impersonation (impersonation). An attacker impersonates a trusted person or company employee to gain access to information or systems.

Tailgating. An intruder enters a protected premises by following a legitimate user in order to gain physical access to protected areas or information.

Social engineering and manipulation pose a serious threat to the security of information and systems because these techniques rely on exploiting human gullibility and inattention. However, regular training, awareness raising, use of sophisticated security measures and monitoring of suspicious activity can significantly reduce the risk of successful attacks and protect both individual users and organisations.

Threats to privacy and confidentiality in today's digital world are becoming increasingly significant, affecting both individual users and organisations. These threats can come from a variety of sources, including cybercriminals, companies that collect data, and even government agencies [19]. Let us consider the main types of threats, their consequences and ways to protect ourselves.

Cyberattacks and hacking. Attackers hack into systems and networks to steal data, which can lead to the leakage of personal and financial information, data loss, and financial losses.

Surveillance and monitoring. Collecting data about users without their knowledge leads to violation of privacy, use of data without consent, possibility of blackmail.

Data Leaks. Illegal or accidental access to personal data has consequences in the form of massive leaks of confidential information, compromising personal and financial data.

Data collection by companies. Companies collect and analyse user data for marketing purposes through social media and analysis of consumer preferences, resulting in privacy violations, use of data without users' explicit consent.

Threats to data privacy and confidentiality in the digital world are multifaceted and can have serious consequences. Effective protection requires an integrated approach that includes technical, educational, legal and procedural measures. This will significantly reduce risks and provide a higher level of security for users and organisations.

The above-mentioned types of threats to personal information security emphasise the importance of a comprehensive approach to data protection, including not only technical measures, but also raising users' awareness of possible risks and methods to prevent them.

2.2. PSYCHOLOGICAL AND SOCIAL ASPECTS OF INFORMATION THREATS

Information threats, such as cyberattacks, data breaches and cyberbullying, can have a significant impact on the ***psychological well-being of individuals***. Let us consider the main aspects of this impact.

Stress and anxiety. The constant threat of cyberattacks and identity leaks can cause chronic stress and anxiety, which has a negative impact on mental health.

Feelings of vulnerability and powerlessness. An individual may feel a sense of helplessness and vulnerability knowing that their personal data may be stolen or used without their consent.

Depression and loss of self-esteem. Cyberbullying and online attacks can lead to depression and loss of self-esteem, especially in young people and adolescents who are more susceptible to social media.

Information threats can contribute to the ***social isolation of an individual***. Let us consider the main mechanisms of this process.

Loss of trust in online communication. Ongoing security threats and incidents can lead to an individual avoiding the use of online platforms for communication, which limits their social contacts.

Isolation due to cyberbullying. Victims of cyberbullying may choose to isolate themselves as a way to avoid further attacks, leading to social rejection and loneliness.

Stigmatisation and discrimination. Leaking confidential information can lead to stigmatisation and discrimination in the real world, which also contributes to social exclusion.

Social networks play a key role in the spread and amplification of information threats [20]. Here are some aspects of this influence.

Spreading misinformation. Social media are often used to spread fake news and misinformation, which can cause panic and distrust of official sources of information.

Cyberbullying and trolling. Social media provides a platform for anonymous cyberbullying and trolling, which can have a serious impact on users' mental health.

Data collection and use. Social networks actively collect user data, which can be used both for targeted advertising and for more malicious purposes such as social engineering and opinion manipulation.

These psychological and social aspects of information threats emphasise the need for a comprehensive approach to personal protection in the information society. This includes both technological measures and the development of information literacy and psychological resilience in users.

2.3. ETHICAL ISSUES AND INFORMATION SECURITY

Ethical dilemmas in the field of information security are complex situations in which the actions or decisions of professionals may lead to contradictions between different moral principles and professional obligations [21]. Let us consider several such dilemmas.

1 The ethical dilemma between **privacy** and **security** in the field of information security relates to the tension between the need to protect society and infrastructure from threats and the duty to respect the privacy and confidentiality of users. Let us examine this dilemma in more detail.

Privacy refers to users' rights to *privacy* (people have the right to privacy and freedom from unwarranted interference in their personal lives), *data confidentiality* (personal data should be protected from unauthorised access and use), *awareness* and consent (users should be informed about and consent to how their data is collected, used and protected).

Security is designed to protect *national security* (protecting the state *and* society from threats such as terrorism, cyber-attacks and crime), *corporate security (protecting* organisations from data breaches, financial loss and reputational damage), and personal security (protecting individuals from identity theft, fraud and other types of abuse).

Using case studies, consider the ethical dilemma between privacy and security and approaches to resolving it.

Monitoring and data collection. Public security services and private companies can collect and analyse large amounts of data to identify potential threats. This can include tracking internet activity, phone calls and financial transactions. On the one hand, such monitoring can prevent crime and protect society. On the other hand, it violates the privacy of users who may not realise they are being monitored.

Encryption and law enforcement. Companies such as Apple and Google are implementing strong encryption methods to protect user data. This type of encryption protects user privacy, but can also make it more difficult for law enforcement to access data as part of investigations. Requirements to provide "back doors" into encryption systems can weaken overall security.

Access control and employee monitoring. Organisations implement monitoring systems to prevent insider threats and enforce security policies. Employee monitoring can identify potential threats and protect the organisation, but it can also invade employees' privacy and undermine their trust.

Here are various approaches to solving the dilemma.

Transparency. Organisations should be transparent in their data collection and use practices, informing users and employees about what data is collected and for what purpose.

Consent and control. Users must be able to give informed consent to the collection and use of their data and have control over their personal data.

Data minimisation. Collect and store only the data needed for specific purposes, and delete data when it is no longer needed.

Balance of interests. Find a balance between the need for security and respect for privacy rights. This may include developing and implementing technologies that provide security without significantly compromising privacy.

Ethical codes and regulations. Adherence to ethical standards and legal regulations that set the framework for acceptable data collection and use.

The ethical dilemma between privacy and security requires a balanced approach and a constant search for compromise. Information security professionals must strive to create systems that both protect society from threats and respect individuals' rights to privacy.

2 The ethical dilemma of **vulnerability disclosure** arises when someone discovers a vulnerability in software, a security system or any other technological product and is faced with the choice of what to do with that information. Let us consider the main aspects of this dilemma.

Disclosure of the vulnerability to the vendor (responsible disclosure). The vendor gets the opportunity to fix the vulnerability, protecting users and their data, but the vendor may ignore or delay the fixing process, leaving the vulnerability open for a long time.

Full public disclosure (full disclosure). Accelerates the fixing of the vulnerability, as users can demand that the vendor fix the problem quickly and public pressure favours security. However, attackers can exploit the vulnerability before it is patched, which can lead to significant losses and data compromise.

Non-disclosure (hiding information). The vulnerability does not become known to the general public, which may reduce the likelihood of exploitation by attackers, but the vulnerability remains unpatched and potentially dangerous to users.

Here are various approaches to solving the dilemma.

Responsible Disclosure Model. The vendor should be informed of the problem and given a certain amount of time to fix it before public disclosure. This approach balances the need for remediation with reducing the risk of attackers exploiting the vulnerability.

Communicating with the professional community. Involving security experts to discuss and work out the best solution can help to find the best approach.

Legal aspects. First of all, it is necessary to take into account the legislation related to vulnerability disclosure in order not to violate legal regulations.

Thus, vulnerability disclosure is a complex ethical issue that requires balancing different interests and possible consequences. The best approach is often the responsible disclosure model, which allows the vendor to fix the problem before it is publicly disclosed, thereby protecting users and contributing to improved product security.

3 The ethical dilemma of **balancing openness and secrecy** often arises in various fields such as business, science, medicine, public administration and others. It is important to realise that this is a conflict between the need to keep certain information secret and the desire for transparency and accessibility of information to the public. Let us consider this dilemma on the example of business and medicine.

BUSINESS	**MEDICINE**
Secrecy	
1. *Competitive advantage.* Companies often keep their strategic plans, new product developments and marketing strategies secret in order to maintain a competitive advantage. 2. *Customer Privacy.* Businesses are required to protect their customers' personal data to avoid leaks and possible misuse. 3. *Internal issues.* Information about internal company issues (e.g. financial difficulties or conflicts between employees) is also often kept confidential so as not to undermine the company's reputation.	1. *Patient confidentiality.* Doctor-patient confidentiality is a fundamental principle that protects patients' personal medical data. *Ethical research.* Some medical research requires secrecy to protect research participants and ensure the objectivity of the results.
Openness	
1. *Customer trust.* Transparency about the use of customer data and honest communication about products and services can build customer trust. 2. *Corporate Social Responsibility.* *Being* open about corporate social responsibility and sustainable development can improve a company's reputation. 3. *Investors* demand transparency in financial statements and strategic plans to make informed decisions.	1. *Public Health.* Transparency regarding epidemiological data and information on the spread of disease is necessary to protect public health. 2. *Scientific research.* Open access to the results of scientific research advances medicine and allows other scientists to verify and use the data.

The balance between openness and secrecy is a complex and multifaceted task, requiring consideration of the interests of different parties and the possible consequences. Each situation is unique, and the approach to resolving this dilemma must be reasoned and balanced, based on ethical principles, legislation and the public interest.

Each of these dilemmas requires careful analysis and a balanced approach that takes into account both professional standards and universal moral principles. Information security professionals should strive to find the best solution while minimising negative consequences for all parties.

Information security is directly linked to **human rights,** including the right to privacy, access to information and freedom of expression.

The right to privacy is a fundamental right that can be undermined by inadequate information security. Measures are needed to protect personal data from unauthorised access and use.

The right of access to information. It is important to ensure that information protection measures do not restrict access to knowledge and information necessary for personal and professional development.

Freedom of expression. Protecting information security should not lead to censorship and restriction of freedom of expression. It is important to strike a balance between preventing malicious activity and protecting the right to expression.

Clear **standards** and norms of behaviour are needed to ensure an ethical approach to information security:

Develop and implement ethical standards. International and national standards governing aspects of information security, such as data collection, storage and use, should be developed.

Ethical behaviour in cyberspace. Promote ethical behaviour among users and IT professionals, including respect for the privacy and rights of other users.

Monitoring and enforcement of standards. Introduce mechanisms to monitor and enforce compliance with ethical standards, including independent audit firms and ethics committees capable of investigating and sanctioning violations.

Ethical issues related to information security require an integrated approach combining legal, technical and moral measures. It is important to consider the multiple dimensions of ethics in the context of digitalisation and globalisation in order to create a safe and just information society.

CHAPTER III. STRATEGIES FOR ENSURING PERSONAL INFORMATION SECURITY

In today's world, personal information security is becoming an increasingly urgent task, given the rapid development of information technologies and the widespread use of digital platforms. Every day a person faces various threats in cyberspace, ranging from personal data leakage to fraud and cyberbullying. In a digitally transformed society, protecting information about each of us is of paramount importance.

With the development of information technology, not only the number and variety of cyber threats are increasing, but also the complexity of methods to protect against them. Traditional approaches to security that worked effectively a few years ago are often insufficient in the face of new challenges. In this regard, the development and implementation of comprehensive information security strategies that cover all aspects of personal protection in the digital space is becoming relevant.

3.1 STATE AND INTERNATIONAL APPROACHES TO INFORMATION SECURITY

State information security policies include many legislative measures aimed at protecting information and critical infrastructure from cyber threats. Let's look at the main aspects of such policies and examples of legislative measures in different countries.

The main aspects of information security policy include:

1. ***Development of national strategies and programmes.*** States develop national cyber security strategies that include goals and priorities for protecting information systems and programmes to improve the cyber resilience of critical infrastructure.

2. ***Establishment of a legal and regulatory framework.*** Legislative acts regulating data protection, cybercrime, and critical infrastructure protection infrastructure, as well as standards and regulations for the private sector on data protection.

3. ***Organisation of specialised bodies and centres.*** National cyber security centres and bodies responsible for coordination and implementation of state policy in this area.

4. ***International co-operation.*** Participation in international agreements and initiatives on cyber security, cooperation with other countries and international organisations in the fight against cyber crime.

Here are examples of legislative measures in different countries in the field of information security.

Uzbekistan

The Law of the Republic of Uzbekistan "On Informatisation" (No. 560-II of 11.12.2003) regulates relations in the field of informatisation, use of information resources and information systems, establishes obligations to protect information and liability for its illegal use.

The Law of the Republic of Uzbekistan "On Personal Data" (No. ZRU-547 of 02.07.2019) regulates relations in the field of personal data arising from the processing and protection of personal data, regardless of the means of processing applied, including information technologies.

The Law of the Republic of Uzbekistan "On Cyber Security" (No. ZRU-764 of 15.04.2022) regulates relations in the field of cyber security and defines the protection of the interests of individuals, society and the state from external and internal threats in cyberspace as a priority in ensuring the cyber security of the state.

Legislative measures in the area of information security in Uzbekistan are aimed at creating a comprehensive information protection system, including both legal and technical aspects that ensure the protection of data and information systems at all levels.

Russian Federation

The Federal Law "On Personal Data" (No. 152-FZ of 27.07.2006) regulates the collection, storage and processing of personal data and establishes requirements for the protection of personal data from unauthorised access.

The Federal Law "On the Security of Critical Information Infrastructure of the Russian Federation" (No. 187-FZ of 26.07.2017) regulates the protection of critical information infrastructure from cyberattacks and introduces obligations for owners of critical information infrastructure objects to ensure their security.

U.S.A.

Federal Information Security Management Act (FISMA, 2002) is a law to protect federal government information systems and establishes standards and requirements for information security management in federal agencies.

The Cybersecurity Information Sharing Act (CISA, 2015) is a private sector-government cyber threat information sharing law and provides a legal framework for sharing cyber threat information to prevent and combat cyber attacks.

European Union

The NIS Directive (2016) is a directive on the security of networks and information systems that obliges EU member states to establish national cybersecurity strategies and requires operators of essential services and digital service providers to adopt risk and incident management measures.

The General Data Protection Regulation (GDPR, 2016) is a general data protection regulation that governs the processing and protection of personal data of EU citizens and includes requirements for data security and notification of data security breaches.

States' information security policies include a wide range of measures aimed at protecting information and critical infrastructure. These measures include the development of national strategies, the establishment of legal and regulatory frameworks, the organisation of specialised bodies and international co-operation. Examples of legislative measures from different countries demonstrate the diversity of approaches and tools used to ensure information security at the national level.

International information security *agreements* and *standards* play an important role in protecting data and infrastructures on a global scale. They establish common principles and procedures for information security and data exchange between countries and organisations. The following are key international agreements and standards in this area.

International agreements

1. ***The Computer Crime Convention*** (Council of Europe Convention on Cybercrime CETS No. 185) (Budapest, 23 November 2001) is the first international agreement aimed at combating crime in cyberspace. It covers issues related to computer-related offences, including illegal access, interference with data and systems, as well as content-related offences and copyright infringement.

2.***The UN Convention on Combating the Use of Information and Communication Technologies for Criminal Purposes*** (also known as the UN Convention on Cybercrime) aims to combat offences related to the use of information and communication technologies. The main objectives and principles of this convention include:

Defining and criminalising cybercrime: developing commonly accepted definitions for various types of cybercrime, such as computer fraud, data theft, malware distribution, hacking and other forms of illegal online activity; establishing obligations for States parties to criminalise certain acts in national legislation.

Cooperation between States: strengthening international cooperation in combating cybercrime, including information exchange, joint investigations and extradition; establishing mechanisms for the rapid and effective exchange of data between law enforcement agencies of different countries.

Measures to prevent cybercrime: developing and implementing measures to prevent cybercrime, including raising public awareness and improving cybersecurity; training and capacity building for law enforcement and judicial officials on cybersecurity and cybercrime.

Protection of human rights and fundamental freedoms: ensuring respect for human rights and fundamental freedoms in the development and application of measures to counter cybercrime; guaranteeing respect for the principle of legality, proportionality and necessity in the investigation and prosecution of cybercrime.

The Convention was developed in response to the growing threats posed by the use of information and communications technologies for criminal purposes and the need for a global legal framework to combat cybercrime. It emphasises the importance of international cooperation and coordination of efforts between different countries to effectively combat this type of crime.

3. ***The UN Convention on International Information Security* is** a framework agreement aimed at establishing common norms and principles to ensure security in cyberspace. It is being developed in the context of growing threats to information security, such as cyberattacks, cyber espionage, the spread of malicious software and other forms of cybercrime. The UN Convention on International Information Security seeks to create a unified legal and regulatory space for combating cyber threats and ensuring security in the information sphere. This initiative plays a key role in shaping a sustainable and secure global information environment that meets modern challenges and threats.

International standards

1.   ISO/IEC 27001 is an international standard for information security management systems (ISMS) adopted in 2013. It defines the

requirements for the creation, implementation, maintenance and continuous improvement of ISMS, which helps organisations to protect their information resources.

2.   ISO/IEC 27002 is a guide to information security management that provides practical guidance on information security management measures. It provides a set of controls that can be used to implement an ISMS based on ISO/IEC 27001.

3. NIST SP 800-53 is a standard developed by the U.S. National Institute of Standards and Technology (NIST) that offers guidance for managing the security of federal agency information systems. Includes recommendations for risk management and protective measures to ensure the security of information systems.

4. GDPR (General Data Protection Regulation) adopted in 2016 and entered into force in 2018, regulates the processing of personal data of individuals in the European Union. It establishes strict rules on data protection and privacy, including requirements for notification of data security breaches.

These agreements and standards help to create a coherent approach to information security at the international level, facilitating co-operation between countries and organisations and promoting better protection of information on a global scale.

3.2. TECHNOLOGICAL MEASURES AND TOOLS TO ENSURE INFORMATION SECURITY

Modern information security **technologies** encompass a variety of methods and tools aimed at ensuring the security of data and systems. Let's take a closer look at the key information security technologies.

1. **Encryption** is the process of converting information into a form that cannot be read by outsiders. Let's consider the main types of encryption.

Symmetric encryption uses a single key to encrypt and decrypt data.

Examples of algorithms: AES (Advanced Encryption Standard), DES (Data Encryption Standard).

Asymmetric encryption uses two keys - a public key for encryption and a private key for decryption. Examples of algorithms: RSA (Rivest-Shamir-Adleman), ECC (Elliptic Curve Cryptography).

Hybrid encryption is a combination of symmetric and asymmetric encryption, often used in security protocols such as TLS (Transport Layer Security).

2. **Authentication** is the process of verifying the authenticity of a user or device. The main methods are:

Password authentication is a method of protecting information and systems from unauthorised access through the use of passwords, which method is widespread and is one of the main ways to ensure security in digital systems.

Two-factor authentication (2FA) requires the use of two methods to prove identity (e.g., a password and a one-time code sent to your phone).

Biometric authentication requires the use of unique biological characteristics such as fingerprints, facial or iris recognition.

Certificate-based authentication involves the use of digital certificates to prove identity.

3. **Authorisation** is the process of granting a user or device access rights to resources after successful authentication. Authorisation methods include: *role-based access control* (RBAC), where access is granted based on the user's roles in the organisation and *attribute-based access control* (ABAC), where access is granted based on attributes of the user, resources and the environment.

4. **Malware protection** is a set of technologies and methods aimed at detecting, preventing and removing malicious software (viruses, Trojans, worms, etc.). Its main components include.

Signature analysis - comparing files against a database of known malware.

Heuristic analysis - analysis of program behaviour to detect potentially malicious code.

Sandboxing - running suspicious programs in an isolated environment to analyse their behaviour.

Real-time monitoring - track system activity and prevent suspicious activity.

5. **Firewalls** are devices or software that monitor and filter network traffic based on specified security rules. Types of firewalls:

Packet filters - filters traffic based on IP addresses and ports.

Application-level firewalls - analyse data at the application level, providing deeper inspection.

Next Generation Firewalls (NGFW) - include additional features such as SSL inspection, intrusion prevention (IPS), and application control.

6. Access Control Systems determine who can use which resources and what resources can be used. They include:

Identity and Access Management (IAM) *systems* - centralised management of users and their access rights.

Mandated Access Control (MAC) - Access is granted based on predefined policies set by the administrator.

Discretionary Access Control (DAC) - resource owners determine who has what access rights.

Together, these technologies provide multiple layers of information security to help prevent unauthorised access and protect data from a variety of threats.

Specialised software for information protection and security management plays a key role in modern information systems. Here is a brief overview of its main categories.

1. **Antivirus programmes** are designed to detect, prevent and remove malicious programmes (viruses, worms, Trojans, etc.). Examples: Kaspersky Anti-Virus, Norton AntiVirus, McAfee.

2. **Anti-spyware programmes** focus on detecting and removing spyware that can collect information about the user without their knowledge. Examples: Spybot Search & Destroy, Malwarebytes.

3. **Information security management** (SIEM) **systems** help organisations collect, analyse and monitor security events in real time. SIEM systems combine data from various sources and provide centralised security management. Examples: Splunk, IBM QRadar, ArcSight.

4. **Data encryption software** can perform both *full disc encryption* to protect data in case of theft or loss of the device (Examples: BitLocker, VeraCrypt) and *file and folder encryption* to protect data during transmission or storage (Examples: AxCrypt, 7-Zip).

5. **Identity and Access Management** (IAM) **solutions** manage access to resources and data based on user identification and rights. Examples: Microsoft Azure AD, Okta, CyberArk.

6. **Multi-factor authentication** (MFA) is used to enhance security by using multiple authentication factors. Examples: Google Authenticator, Duo Security.

7. **Data Leakage Protection** (DLP) **solutions** prevent sensitive information from leaking outside the organisation by controlling and restricting the transfer of data. DLP solutions can analyse data in motion, at rest, and in use. Examples: Symantec DLP, McAfee Total Protection for Data Loss Prevention, Forcepoint DLP.

These tools and systems play an important role in securing information systems and protecting data from various threats and leaks.

The development of information security technologies is a critical challenge for protecting data and infrastructure from cyber threats. Here is a brief overview of **promising trends** in this area:

1. **Artificial intelligence and machine learning.**

Automate threat detection. Machine learning algorithms can analyse large volumes of data to identify anomalies and potential threats, significantly reducing incident response times.

Predictive analytics. AI helps predict potential attacks based on previous data and current cyber threat trends.

Adaptive defence. AI systems can dynamically adapt to new threats, improving network and data protection.

2. **Blockchain.**

Decentralised data storage. Blockchain provides a high level of data protection due to its distributed architecture, which makes it resistant to attacks and hacking [22].

Secure Transactions. Blockchain smart contracts and cryptographic algorithms ensure secure and transparent transactions.

Identity protection. Using blockchain for identity management can significantly reduce the risks of fraud and identity theft.

3. **Quantum encryption.**

Resistance to quantum attacks. Quantum encryption uses the laws of quantum mechanics to create unbreakable keys, making it resistant to attacks by quantum computers.

Data transmission with absolute security. Quantum Key Distribution (QKD) protocols ensure that any attempts to intercept data are detected, providing a high level of security for critical communications.

4. **Internet of Things (IoT).**

Inbuilt security mechanisms. Develop IoT devices with inbuilt security features such as data encryption and authentication.

Network Segmentation. Use technology to segment IoT devices into separate networks, reducing the risk of attack propagation.

Monitoring and management. Advanced monitoring systems that use AI to analyse the behaviour of IoT devices and prevent anomalies.

Each of these areas presents significant opportunities to improve information security. The adoption and development of these technologies will help create more secure and cyber-resilient systems, providing reliable protection for data and infrastructure across industries.

3.3. EDUCATIONAL AND CULTURAL ASPECTS OF INFORMATION SECURITY

Education plays a key role in information security at various levels, from general secondary education to postgraduate education. Let us consider each of these areas in more detail [23].

1. **General secondary and specialised secondary education.** At the level of general secondary and secondary specialised education, the basic knowledge and skills necessary to understand and comply with the rules of information security are laid down. Let us take a closer look at the most important aspects.

Awareness. Students are explained basic information security concepts such as cyber threats, data privacy and how to protect personal information.

Security Skills. Learning how to work safely on the Internet, how to use strong passwords, awareness of phishing attacks and malware.

Ethics on the Internet. Promote responsible and ethical online behaviour, including respect for others' privacy and intellectual property.

2. **Higher education** plays a more significant role in this aspect, providing students with specialised knowledge and skills in the field of information security. The introduction of the discipline "Media Literacy and Information Culture" into the curricula of humanitarian areas of higher education is an urgent and important task. This discipline will help students to understand the basic principles of information security, as well as to develop critical thinking and information analysis skills, and will help

students not only to better navigate in the modern information space, but also to protect themselves from a variety of threats associated with the use of digital technologies [24].

Undergraduate programmes. Higher education institutions offer information security and cybersecurity programmes that train professionals in this field [25].

Master's programmes. Specialised master's programmes that train cybersecurity experts allow students to focus on specialised aspects of information security, such as cryptography, malware analysis and risk management.

Research. Students and faculty members participate in research aimed at developing new methods for protecting information and countering cyber threats.

Practical skills. Students undergo practical training and internships in IT companies, where they apply the acquired knowledge in practice.

3. **Postgraduate education** in the field of information security comprises two main levels: *basic doctoral* (postgraduate) and *doctoral studies.* Both levels are aimed at in-depth study and research of information security issues, but they have different objectives and requirements.

The basic doctorate (postgraduate) and *doctoral studies* differ in the level of training and expected results, but both levels contribute to professional growth and career development in the scientific and industrial fields of information security.

Postgraduate education in information security provides in-depth knowledge and skills for research and development of new technologies.

4. **Training and professional development** allow existing specialists to constantly update their knowledge and skills in the rapidly changing field of information security: *certification programmes such* as CISSP, CEH, CISM provide in-depth knowledge and validation of

specialists' qualifications; *refresher courses* update specialists' knowledge and skills in accordance with the latest technologies and protection methods.

5. **Educational campaigns and public initiatives** play an important role in raising general awareness of information security issues among the public.

Public campaigns are aimed at informing a wide audience about the basic principles of information security.

Community initiatives include volunteer programmes, seminars and webinars run by community organisations and IT companies for different groups of people.

Resources and tools are provided free of charge for information security training (online courses, articles, videos, etc.).

Thus, education at all levels plays a critical role in information security by building basic and specialised knowledge, developing skills and keeping competencies in this critical area up-to-date.

Cultural aspects play an important role in the perception of information security. Each culture has its own unique values, ideas about privacy, and attitudes toward technology [26]. Let us consider several cultural factors that may influence perceptions of information security.

Privacy is the right to personal freedom and control over one's own information. The protection of privacy ensures individual autonomy by preserving personal space and respecting privacy. The right to privacy is protected by law in many countries and there are various standards and regulations governing the collection, use and transfer of personal data. However, in light of the rapid development of technology and digital services, new challenges to protecting privacy are emerging, and ongoing work in this area remains important. Different cultures have different ideas about what constitutes personal information and how it should be protected.

In cultures where *individualism* prevails, such as Western countries, privacy and personal freedom are generally valued more highly. People expect their personal data to be protected and not used without their consent. In cultures with a *collectivist mentality,* such as some Asian countries, there may be a more widespread understanding that personal privacy should be subordinated to the interests of the community or group.

Some *religious* and *cultural* beliefs can also shape perceptions of privacy. For example, some cultures in Islam and Orthodoxy have strict rules about women's privacy and family life.

In *modern developed societies* where digital technology and social media are pervasive, new questions about data privacy may arise. In such cultures, people may be more aware of their privacy rights and more demanding in protecting their personal data.

These factors can lead to differences in privacy legislation, data protection standards in relation to the handling of personal information in different cultures.

Attitudes towards technology*.* The level of technological literacy and attitudes towards technological innovation can also vary across cultures. Attitudes towards technology are also very diverse and depend on many factors such as personal experience, cultural context, education and even psychological characteristics.

Some people perceive technology as a means to improve the quality of life and empowerment. They actively use new technologies in everyday life, considering them indispensable assistants.

Other people may be more cautious or even sceptical about technology because of concerns about privacy, security or the impact on social relationships. They may prefer to keep some distance from new technologies or to study them more carefully before participating in their use.

In any case, technology is becoming an increasingly integral part of our lives, and it is important to maintain a balance between using technology to achieve your goals and using it in an informed way to avoid possible negative consequences.

Ethical and moral beliefs can also influence perceptions of information security. For example, some cultures may consider it unacceptable to violate privacy, even if it is necessary for security purposes.

Understanding these cultural aspects helps to develop more effective information security strategies, taking into account the unique needs and preferences of different cultural groups.

Information literacy encompasses a wide range of skills and knowledge that are necessary to effectively find, evaluate, use and manage information [27]. In today's digital world, these skills are critical to personal security. Let us consider three key aspects: critical thinking skills, knowledge of digital security, and ethical use of information.

1. Critical thinking is the ability to objectively analyse and evaluate information to form valid conclusions. In the context of information literacy, critical thinking helps to effectively address the following tasks.

Determining the credibility of information sources is an important task in the process of dealing with information, whether it is research, journalism or just everyday news consumption. The following are the main methods for determining the credibility of sources, with examples.

Determining the author's credibility by checking the *author's* qualifications, experience and reputation. For example, an article on medical research written by an MD with years of experience and publications in scientific journals is more likely to be credible.

Analysing the source of the publication. Check the reputation of the publication or platform where the information was published. For example, a scientific article published in a peer-reviewed journal will usually be more credible than an article on a personal blog.

Citation verification. Analysing the number of times a paper has been cited by other authoritative sources. For example, a paper that is frequently cited in other scientific articles has a high citation index and is considered reliable.

Analysing evidence and methodology. Checking whether a source uses evidence-based methodology and reliable data. For example, a study conducted using control groups and statistically significant data will be considered more credible.

Comparison with other sources. Comparing information with data from other reliable sources to confirm facts. For example, news confirmed by several major news outlets is more reliable.

Objectivity test. An assessment of whether an author or publication has a bias or conflict of interest. For example, information provided by independent think tanks is generally considered more objective than material sponsored by vested interests.

Use of verified factchecking platforms. Verify information using specialised fact-checking websites and platforms. For example, information verified by organisations such as Snopes or FactCheck.org will be more reliable.

Reverse source checking. Checking the original sources to which the information refers. For example, if a news story refers to a scientific study, it is important to check the study itself to ensure the accuracy of the data presented.

Contextuality check. An assessment of the context in which information is presented to avoid taking data out of context. For example, statistics presented with the full context of the study will be more reliable than those presented without an explanation of the underlying conditions.

These methods allow you to evaluate information more critically and select the most credible sources for your work or personal use.

Information analysis and synthesis are important methodological approaches used for knowledge acquisition, problem solving and decision making. They are often used in scientific research, business intelligence, engineering, and other fields. Let's take a closer look at each of these methodologies and give examples of their application.

Information analysis is the process of decomposing complex information or a system into simpler component parts in order to examine and understand them. Analysis helps to identify key elements and their interrelationships.

Let's define the main stages of information analysis: 1) Determining the purpose and objectives of the analysis. 2) Collecting information. 3) Dividing the information into its constituent parts. 4) Studying each part separately. 5) Identifying the relationships between the parts. 6) Formulating conclusions.

Suppose a company wants to understand the reasons for declining sales.

1) *Target definition.* To find out the reasons for declining sales.

2) *Information Gathering.* Collect data on sales, marketing campaigns, economic conditions, customer feedback, etc.

3) *Separation of information.* Categorise data into categories, e.g. by time, products, regions, sales channels.

4) *Examining the parts.* Analysing each category separately. For example, examining sales data by region.

5) *Identifying correlations.* Identify correlations between lower sales and, for example, lower marketing costs or economic downturns in certain regions.

6) *Formulating conclusions.* Identify specific reasons, such as reduced advertising budget or negative customer feedback.

Synthesising information is the process of combining separate pieces of information into a whole to arrive at an overall view or solution. Synthesis helps to integrate different aspects and gain a holistic understanding.

Let's define the main stages of information synthesis: 1) Determining the purpose and objectives of synthesis. 2) Collecting the necessary parts of information. 3) Analysing each piece of information. 4) Determining the relationships between the parts. 5) Integrating the parts into a whole. 6) Formulating an overall conclusion or decision.

Suppose a company wants to develop a new marketing strategy.

1) *Defining the objective.* Developing an effective marketing strategy.

2) *Gathering pieces of information.* Data on current marketing campaigns, competitor analyses, market research, customer feedback.

3) *Part Analysis.* Analysing data on current campaigns, examining competitor strategies, understanding customer needs.

4)   *Identifying the interrelationships.* Identifying how different marketing approaches affect different market segments.

5)   *Integration.* Combining all pieces of information to create an overall strategy.

6) *Conclusion Formulation.* Creating a comprehensive marketing strategy that takes into account the best practices of competitors, customer needs and analyses current campaigns.

Analysis and synthesis methodologies are often used together. For example, in scientific research, data are first analysed to identify key aspects and patterns, and then a general theory or model is synthesised based on the findings.

Analysis and synthesis are complementary methodologies that help to structure and interpret information. Applying these approaches allows you to effectively solve complex problems and make informed decisions.

2. **Digital security** (or information security) is a set of measures and practices aimed at protecting information systems, networks, data and devices from digital attacks, unauthorised access, cyber threats, damage and theft. The goal of digital security is to ensure the confidentiality, integrity and availability of information.

Key aspects of digital security include *confidentiality, integrity* and *availability.*

Confidentiality is the principle that information to which access is restricted should not be disclosed or used without authorisation. It covers many aspects of human and social life.

Protecting *personal information* such as name, address, phone numbers, medical records, financial data, etc. The importance of protecting this information is heightened in the digital and internet age.

Confidentiality of *commercial data* and *secrets,* which may include business plans, financial information, development strategy, etc. This information is often protected by non-disclosure agreements.

Confidentiality in *professional settings,* such as between doctor and patient, lawyer and client, priest and parishioner. Breach of this confidentiality can lead to legal consequences and loss of trust.

Measures to *protect information* from unauthorised access, alteration and destruction, which includes the use of encryption, access control, regular software updates and staff training.

Laws and regulations *governing the protection of* sensitive information. Different countries have their own data protection laws, such as GDPR in Europe or HIPAA in the United States.

Privacy is important to ensure personal safety, protect rights and freedoms, maintain trust and uphold professional ethics. In today's world, where data is increasingly accessible and vulnerable, privacy issues are becoming increasingly important.

Data and systems ***integrity*** is a principle aimed at ensuring the accuracy, completeness and continuity of information and processes. Integrity includes several key aspects:

Data and systems must be protected from *unauthorised modification*, preventing modifications that could disrupt systems or distort information.

Data must be *accurate* and *reliable,* which is important to make the right decisions based on correct information.

Data must remain *unchanged* during transmission over the network and when stored on various media, which requires the use of technologies such as checksums and hashing to verify that data has not been altered.

It is important to monitor *access* and *changes to* data so that unauthorised actions can be detected and prevented, which includes logging and regular security audits.

Regular data *backups* and the *ability to restore* data in the event of loss or corruption ensure business continuity and minimise loss.

Develop and implement clear *policies* and *procedures* that govern who can *make changes to* data and systems and how, helping to avoid accidental errors and misuse.

The integrity of data and systems is critical to ensuring their reliability and trustworthiness. In fields ranging from finance and healthcare to government and information technology, maintaining integrity is a key component of overall security and resilience.

Data and systems ***availability*** is an information security principle that ensures that information and services are available to users at the right time and place. This principle means that data and services should be available to the extent required to fulfil business processes or meet user needs.

Systems need to be designed for *failure* and *resilience.* Redundancy, data backups and automatic recovery mechanisms help minimise downtime and ensure continuous availability.

Systems must be ready to *scale to* ensure availability even as the load or user base grows. Horizontal scaling and the use of cloud technologies allow resources to scale efficiently as needed.

To ensure availability, data and services must operate at *high* response *rates,* which requires optimisation of system architecture, network infrastructure and data processes.

Protecting against DDoS attacks, viruses and other types of cyber threats is also part of ensuring availability. Implementing defences such as firewalls, firewalls and intrusion detection systems can help prevent attacks aimed at restricting access.

Regular *maintenance* and *updates to* systems and software are essential to prevent unplanned downtime and ensure reliable operation.

Backing up your data and developing disaster *recovery plans* helps reduce downtime and ensure rapid restoration of availability.

Ensuring accessibility is a key aspect in ensuring that businesses operate efficiently and that users' needs are met. Accessibility violations can lead to serious consequences such as loss of customers, reputational damage and financial loss.

Digital security methods and tools can include anti-virus software, firewalls, data encryption, access control systems, security auditing and monitoring, training and user awareness.

3. ethical **use of information** is the observance of moral principles and standards in the collection, storage, processing, dissemination and use of data. The main aspects of ethical use of information include:

Privacy. Protecting personal data and information from unauthorised access, which is particularly important when dealing with personal data where a breach of confidentiality can have serious consequences for individuals.

Transparency. Open and honest communication about how data is collected, stored and used, which includes notifying users of the purpose of data collection and how it is used.

Consent. Obtaining explicit consent for the collection and use of data. People should be able to control what their data is collected and how it will be used.

Intended use. Use the data exclusively for the stated purposes and avoid using it in other contexts without authorisation.

Accuracy. Ensuring that data is accurate, complete and up-to-date, which is important for making informed decisions and preventing the dissemination of false information.

Security. Protecting data from leaks, losses and other threats such as hacker attacks, which includes implementing technical and organisational measures to ensure data security.

Fairness. Avoiding discrimination and unfair treatment in the use of data. This is important to avoid bias and inequality in data-driven decision-making.

Liability. Having clearly defined responsibility for the processing of data and the consequences of its use. Organisations and individuals working with data should be held accountable for ethical behaviour.

Applying these principles helps to ensure that information is handled fairly and responsibly, that human rights are respected and that trust between organisations and the public is built.

The educational and cultural aspects discussed above emphasise the importance of a comprehensive approach to the development of personal information security, including not only technological measures, but also the formation of appropriate knowledge, skills and cultural attitudes.

The concept of information security has undergone a significant evolution due to the development of technology and changes in society. Philosophical approaches, such as phenomenology and critical theory, help to gain a deeper understanding of the nature of information threats and their impact on the individual.

Cyberattacks, social engineering and privacy threats pose serious risks to the information security of individuals. These threats have not only a technical aspect, but also a psychological and social aspect, affecting the mental health and social relationships of individuals.

Ethical and legal issues play an important role in shaping approaches to information security. The balance between security and human rights, such as the right to privacy and freedom of expression, requires careful consideration and adherence to ethical standards.

Effective information security measures require coordination at the state and international levels. State policies, international agreements and standards, and the role of international organisations are key components of a successful strategy.

Based on the study, the following **recommendations** can be made:

Awareness raising and educational programmes. Introduce cyber security courses in school and university programmes, as well as training for employees. It is also important to launch public campaigns aimed at raising awareness of risks and methods of protection.

Improving legislation and international co-operation. Developing and adopting laws aimed at data protection and combating cybercrime, and actively participating in international agreements and initiatives. Establishing international standards and protocols for joint response to threats.

Development and implementation of new technologies. Investing in the development and implementation of advanced technologies such as quantum cryptography, blockchain and artificial intelligence to improve data protection and prevent attacks.

Supporting ethical standards. Developing and enforcing ethical standards for information security, including protecting human rights and ensuring fair access to information. Establish ethics committees and independent auditors to monitor and enforce standards.

Shaping cultural values and norms. Promoting a culture of information security, including respect for privacy, risk awareness and responsible behaviour in the digital space. Participate in international cultural exchanges and initiatives to improve digital literacy.

These recommendations will help create a safer information society where personal information is secure and users have the knowledge and skills to deal with today's threats.

The study of personal information security in the information society has revealed several **promising directions** for further philosophical and interdisciplinary research:

Ethics and Artificial Intelligence. Explores ethical issues related to the use of artificial intelligence in information security, including aspects of privacy, autonomy and trust.

Philosophy of technology and digital identity. Analysing the impact of new technologies on the notion of personhood and identity in the digital space. How digital footprints and behavioural data affect the perception of personhood and identity.

Cyberphilosophy and Posthumanism. An exploration of the concepts of posthumanism in the context of information security, including the impact of cyberspace on human experience and essence.

Interdisciplinary approaches to cyber security. Combining philosophy with computer science, sociology, psychology and law for a more comprehensive understanding of information security. Analysis of social and psychological factors that influence user behaviour and threat perception.

Philosophy of law and information security. Examination of the legal aspects of information security from a philosophical perspective. Issues of regulation, respect for human rights and the balance between security and freedoms.

Active public engagement in information security will create a more secure and resilient digital space where everyone can enjoy the benefits of technology without fear of privacy. Working together to promote literacy, advanced technology and ethical behaviour will ensure strong protection in a rapidly changing information world.

LITERATURE

1.   Burnashev R. Philosophical analysis of the concept of information society //Namangan davlat universiteti Ilmiy axborotnomasi. - 2023. - №. 9. - C. 194-202.

2.   Krasnoyarchuk V. I. From the history of the first computer viruses // Theory and practice of financial and economic activity of enterprises of various industries. Science and society: actual problems and solutions. - 2021. - C. 456-460.

3. Klishina Y. E., Uglitskikh O. N. Risks of cyberattacks and insurance of cyberthreats. N. Risks of cyber attacks and insurance of cyber threats //The role of risk management and insurance in ensuring the sustainability of society and economy. - 2023. - C. 195-201.

4. Bulatenko M. A., Goronok D. L. Key problems of ensuring economic security of the enterprise in modern conditions // Vestnik Altai Academy of Economics and Law. - 2019. - №. 2. - C. 71-75.

5. Skudnev D. M. et al. Prospective possibilities of using artificial intelligence to prevent cyberattacks // Modern Science-Intensive Technologies. - 2020. - №. 8. - C. 75-78.

6. Kadochnikov, V. P. Philosophical problems of scientific research of the phenomenon of information (in Russian) // Omsk scientific bulletin. - 2007. - №. 2 (54). - C. 114119.

7.Burnashev R. F. F. F., Asrorova M. O., Masarova K. F. Philosophical foundations of the concept of personal security in the era of digitalisation //Universum: Social Sciences. - 2023. - №. 11 (102). - C. 33-39.

8.Burnashev R. F., Nasimova M. U. Philosophical analysis of transformations of the concept of "love" in the information society //Universum: social sciences. - 2023. - №. 12 (103). - C. 12-18.

9. Burnashev R. F. Analysing the role and place of personality in the

information space //Universum: social sciences. - 2023. - №. 10 (101). - C. 21-26.

10. Burnashev R. F. Virtual World as a New Form of Reality for Man: Philosophical and Psychological Aspects //Journal of Intellectual Property and Human Rights. - 2023. - T. 2. - №. 11. - C. 57-65.

11. Burnashev R. F. Philosophy of information society: problems of social justice in the era of digitalisation //Universum: social sciences. - 2024. - №. 1 (104). - C. 10-14.

12.   Dzhumabaeva M. Sh., Burnashev R. F. Threats of information and psychological security in open information systems //Gospodarka i Innowacje. F. Threats of information and psychological security in open information systems //Gospodarka i Innowacje. - 2023. - T. 35. - C. 794-803.

13. Burnashev R.. F. F., Kholikova M. A. Key aspects and prospects for the use of information technology in business //Universum: Economics and Jurisprudence. - 2023. - №. 7 (106). - C. 4-9.

14. Gokun Y. S. Qualification of hacker attacks under civil legislation //Voprosy Rossiyskaya Justicia. - 2022. - №. 19. - C. 174-179.

15. Kodatsky N. M., Motuz A. C. Cyberattacks analysis and risks // Journal of StudNet. - 2022. - T. 5. - №. 1. - C. 559-566.

16. Lisetsky Y. M., Bobrov S. I. New threats to information security or weapons of mass contamination // Mathematical Machines and Systems. I. New threats to information security or weapons of mass contamination // Mathematical Machines and Systems. - 2018. - №. 1. - C. 41-50.

17.   Dolzhenko I. B. Impact of major risks on the operations of MNCs of the consumer sector //Modern Science. - 2021. - №. 1-2. - C. 42-47.

18.   Burnashev R. F., Murzamuratova U. B. Application of computer linguistics technologies in social networks and Internet marketing

//Universum: philology and art history. - 2023. - №. 10 (112). - C. 14-19.

19. Burnashev R.F., Shavkatova Sh.Sh. Socio-philosophical analysis of digital privacy and its role in ensuring information and psychological security // Universum: Social Sciences. - 2024. - №. 5 (108). - C. 42-46.

20. Burnashev R. F., Khudayberdiyeva M. B. The role of social networks in the transformation of society on the threshold of smart society //Gospodarka i Innowacje. - 2023. - T. 35. - C. 257-263.

21. Burnashev R. F. Philosophical aspects of digital ethics in the era of technological progress //Universum: social sciences. - 2023. - №. 12 (103). - C. 19-23.

22. Burnashev R. F. F., Kurbanova F. H. Blockchain technology: principles of functioning, application and development prospects //Gospodarka i Innowacje. - 2023. - T. 35. - C. 786-793.

23. Burnashev R. F., Makhmudjonova N. M. The role of philosophy in the formation of value orientations in modern education //Universum: Social Sciences. - 2024. - №. 3 (106). - C. 27-31.

24. Burnashev R. F., Makhmudjonova M. D. Philosophical and pedagogical aspects of the development of media literacy in the information society //Universum: social sciences. - 2024. - №. 4 (107). - C. 28-32.

25. Burnashev R. F. Role of innovative technologies in improving the quality of mastering technical sciences //Universum: Technical Sciences. - 2023. - №. 7-1 (112). - C. 14-19.

26. Burnashev R.F., Ismatilloeva M.A. Philosophical analysis of the influence of artificial intelligence on the literature of the era of globalisation // Universum: Social Sciences. - 2024. - №. 5 (108). - C. 47-50.

27. Burnashev R.F., Ziyoeva G.A. Philosophical analysis of media literacy in the context of transformation of information space // Universum: Social Sciences. - 2024. - №. 5 (108). - C. 38-41.

Table of Contents

yes
I want morebooks!

Buy your books fast and straightforward online - at one of world's fastest growing online book stores! Environmentally sound due to Print-on-Demand technologies.

Buy your books online at
www.morebooks.shop

Kaufen Sie Ihre Bücher schnell und unkompliziert online – auf einer der am schnellsten wachsenden Buchhandelsplattformen weltweit! Dank Print-On-Demand umwelt- und ressourcenschonend produzi ert.

Bücher schneller online kaufen
www.morebooks.shop

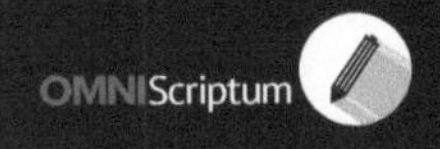

Printed by Books on Demand GmbH, Norderstedt / Germany